MY FIRST

100
ndebele words

Written by Paidamoyo

Copyright © 2020 by Paidamoyo

First edition 2020

All rights reserved. No part of this book may be reproduced or transmitted in any
form or by any means, electronic or mechanical, including photocopying, record-
ing or any information storage or retrieval system without permission from the
copyright holder.

ISBN 978-1779254-641

This book is a Publication of WING UP PUBLISHING

www.winguppublishing.com
info@winguppublishing.com

WING UP
PUBLISHING

Greetings

Sakubona
Hello

Livuka njani
Good Morning

Greetings

Litshona njani?

Good Afternoon

Litshona njani?

Good Evening

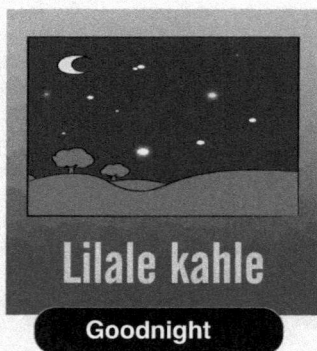

Lilale kahle

Goodnight

Family

UMAMA

UBABA

UMFANA

INKAZANA

UGOGO

UKHULU

Body Parts

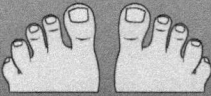

Amazwane

Ikhanda

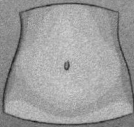

Isisu

Iminwe

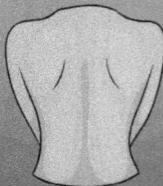

Iqolo

Body Parts

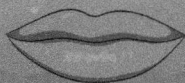

Umlomo

Amazinyo

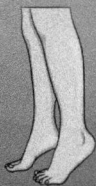

Inyawo

Amehlo

Inzipho

Body Parts

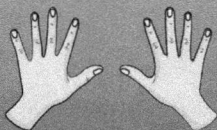
Izandla

Indlebe

Ulimi

Amakhala

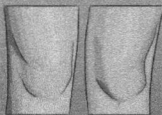
Amadolo

Actions

Ukuthenga

Ukugida

Ukuvuma

Ukwala

Actions

Ukuhleka

Ukukhala

Ukulala

Ukugijima

UKUXHAWULA

Ukuhlala

Ukuma

UKUVALELISA

Ukuthanyela

Ukugezisa

Ukudla

Ukuhlabela

Ukunatha

Ukuhamba

Ukupheka

Animals

IMPISI

Hyena

IGUNDWANE

Mouse

INYONI

Bird

UBHEJANE

Rhinoceros

Animals

IMBUZI

Goat

UMANGOYE

Cat

INDLOVU

Elephant

ISILWANE

Lion

Animals

INKOMO
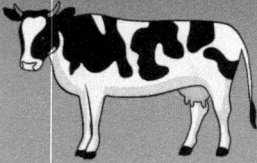
Cow

INJA

Dog

INKAWU

Monkey

IMVU

Sheep

Animals

INKUKHU

Chicken

INYATHI

Buffalo

IDUBE

Zebra

Animals

IXOXO

Frog

INHLANZI

Fish

UMVUNDLA

Rabbit

Animals

INGWE

Leopard

INGULUBE

Pig

IDADA

Duck

Days of the week

Umvulo
①②③④⑤⑥⑦
Monday

Olwesibili
①②③④⑤⑥⑦
Tuesday

Olwesithathu
①②③④⑤⑥⑦
Wednesday

Olwesine
①②③④⑤⑥⑦
Thursday

Days of the week

Olwesihlanu

①②③④⑤⑥⑦

Friday

Umgqibelo

①②③④⑤⑥⑦

Saturday

Isonto

①②③④⑤⑥⑦

Sunday

Months of the year

Uzibandlela

January

Unhlolanja

February

Umbimbitho

March

Umabasa

April

Months of the year

May

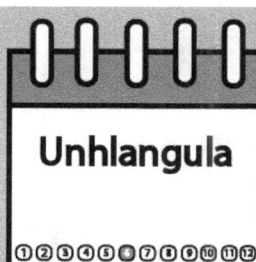

June

July

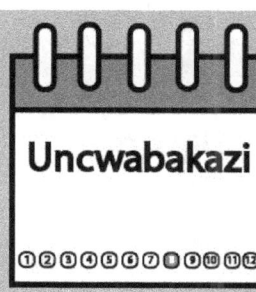

August

Months of the year

Umpandula

① ② ③ ④ ⑤ ⑥ ⑦ ⑧ ⑨ ⑩ ⑪ ⑫

September

Umfumfu

① ② ③ ④ ⑤ ⑥ ⑦ ⑧ ⑨ ⑩ ⑪ ⑫

October

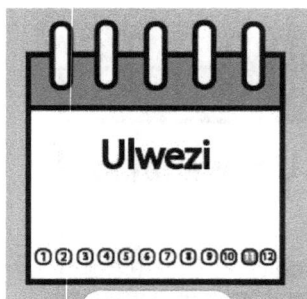

Ulwezi

① ② ③ ④ ⑤ ⑥ ⑦ ⑧ ⑨ ⑩ ⑪ ⑫

November

Umpalakazi

① ② ③ ④ ⑤ ⑥ ⑦ ⑧ ⑨ ⑩ ⑪ ⑫

December

General Information

IZOLO
Yesterday

NAMUHLA
Today

KUSASA
Tomorrow

IKAWUSO

INDLU

IBHULUGWE

INKOMITSHO

UMGANU

IZICATHULO

ITAFULA

IPENSELI

USIBA

ISIGQOKO

UKHEZO

ISITULO

www.ingramcontent.com/pod-product-compliance
Lightning Source LLC
Chambersburg PA
CBHW060604030426
42337CB00019B/3598